UNIVERSITY OF MICHIGAN FOOTBALL TRIVIA

DOUG WEBB

Quinlan Press
Boston

Copyright © 1988
by Doug Webb

All rights reserved,
including the right of reproduction
in whole or in part in any form.
Published by Quinlan Press
131 Beverly Street
Boston, MA 02114

Cover design by Nicole Powers
Cover photograph by Per Kjeldsen

Library of Congress Catalog
Card Number 88-62502
ISBN 1-55770-108-3

Printed in the United States of America

Dedicated to my late father, L. D. Webb, who taught me about sports and life and the relative importance of each. His spirit still lives in those who knew him.

Doug Webb resides in Ann Arbor, Michigan, where he is a project engineer for a land surveying and civil engineering firm. He is also a writer of sports articles, poetry and fiction.

I have attempted to make this book interesting, challenging and, above all, accurate. I wish to thank Sports Guides, Inc., of Ann Arbor, publishers of Michigan Football Guide, especially David DiVarti and Ken Garber, who loaned publications for research and supplied the photos for this book. They also gave freely of their time. Thanks also to photographer Per Kjeldsen for the cover photo and to Jim Harbaugh for his generous permission to use it. I want to extend a very special thanks to my wife, Jan, who encouraged me and built an envelope of peace around me during this project, and to my children, Mike, Wendy and Katie—hugs to each.

Contents

Michigan Offense—Modern Era	
Questions	1
Answers	7
Michigan Defense (1966-1987)	
Questions	11
Answers	15
Individual Records	
Questions	19
Answers	23
Team Single Game Records	
Questions	27
Answers	33
Team Season Records (1938-1987)	
Questions	39
Answers	43
Big Ten Individual Records (1939-1987)	
Questions	47
Answers	59
Big Ten Team Records (1939-1987)	
Questions	69
Answers	77
More Big Ten Trivia	
Questions	83
Answers	89

Big Ten Coaches
   Questions 93
   Answers 95
Michigan vs. The Big Ten and Others
   Questions 97
   Answers 103
Photographs
   Questions 107
   Answers 129
Michigan in Bowl Games
   Questions 131
   Answers 139
Wolverines in the Pro Draft
   Questions 145
   Answers 149

Michigan Offense–Modern Era (1938-1987) Questions

1. What running back gained 347 yards in a single game in 1968?

2. Name the opponent.

3. Name the back who rushed for 253 yards in a contest in 1981.

4. Name the opponent.

5. How many yards did Jamie Morris gain in the 1988 Hall of Fame Bowl?

6. Against which school did he do this?

Michigan Offense—Questions

7. What was the final score of that game?

8. What back once averaged 18.1 yards per carry in a game?

9. Who was the opponent and what year was this accomplished?

10. What was the final score of that game?

11. In the midseventies, what back averaged 18.0 yards per carry in a game?

12. Who was the opponent and what was the score of the game?

13. Who holds the U of M record for most rushing touchdowns in a game?

14. How many did he score?

15. What year did he do this and who was the opponent?

16. Which former back twice scored four touchdowns in a single game?

17. Who were the opponents?

18. How many touchdowns did Rob Lytle score against Indiana in 1975?

19. What was the most yards gained by Jamie Morris in a Big Ten game?

Michigan Offense—Questions

20. What year did he do this and who was the opponent?

21. What former quarterback holds the record for the most passes attempted in a single game?

22. How many did he attempt?

23. What year did he do this and who was the opponent?

24. Who won the game?

25. Who holds the record for the most passes completed in a game?

26. How many did he complete and who was the opponent?

27. Who won the game?

28. Which quarterback completed 21 passes in a 1984 game?

29. Who was the opponent and what was the final score?

30. What was the most passes Jim Harbaugh completed in a game?

31. Against which school did he do this and what was the final score?

32. Which quarterback holds the record for most interceptions thrown in a game?

Michigan Offense—Questions

33. How many did he throw?

34. Who was the opponent?

35. What was the final score?

36. How many career 300-yard games passing did Jim Harbaugh have?

37. What were the totals and who were the opponents?

38. What two Michigan quarterbacks have thrown for four touchdowns in a single contest?

39. Who were the opponents?

40. Who was the last quarterback to throw for three touchdowns in a game?

41. Against which school did he do this?

42. Of the Michigan backs with 500 or more career yards rushing, who is the all-time leader in average yards per game for a single season?

43. What was his average?

44. What year did he accomplish this?

45. What was his total yards gained rushing that year?

Michigan Offense—Questions

46. What was his average gain per carry?

47. Who is the all-time season leader in average gain per carry (minimum 500 yards)?

48. What was his average?

49. What year did he do this?

50. What Michigan back scored 19 rushing touchdowns in a season?

51. Name the year he did this.

52. What was his average yards per game that year?

53. What former quarterback went on to play major league baseball?

54. What organization first signed him to a contract?

Michigan Offense–Modern Era (1938-1987) Answers

1. Ron Johnson

2. Wisconsin

3. Butch Woolfolk

4. Michigan State

5. 234

6. Alabama

7. Michigan 28, Alabama 24

8. Tom Harmon

Michigan Offense—Answers

9. Chicago—1939

10. Michigan 75, Chicago 0

11. Rob Lytle

12. Michigan beat Michigan State, 42-10.

13. Ron Johnson

14. Five

15. 1968—Wisconsin

16. Tom Harmon

17. Iowa (1939) and California (1940)

18. Four

19. 210

20. 1986—Ohio State

21. Dick Vidmer

22. 47

23. 1966—Michigan State

24. MSU, 20-7

25. Bob Ptacek

Michigan Offense—Answers

26. 24, Ohio State

27. OSU, 20-14

28. Chris Zurbrugg

29. Purdue, 31-29

30. 19 (1986)

31. Ohio State, Michigan 26-OSU 24

32. Demetrius Brown

33. Seven

34. MSU (1987)

35. MSU 17, Michigan 11

36. Two

37. 310 against Wisconsin (1986), 300 against Indiana (1986)

38. Steve Smith and Chris Zurbrugg

39. Smith—Purdue (1983), Zurbrugg—Purdue (1984)

40. Demetrius Brown

41. Iowa (1987)

Michigan Offense—Answers

42. Jamie Morris

43. 141.9 yards per game

44. 1987

45. 1,703 (12 games)

46. 6.04 (282 carries)

47. Bill Daley

48. 6.81 yards per carry (120 carries)

49. 1943

50. Ron Johnson

51. 1968

52. 139.1 yards per game

53. Rick Leach

54. Detroit Tigers

Michigan Defense (1966-1987) Questions

1. What Michigan defensive back intercepted ten passes in one year?

2. What year did he do this?

3. How many yards did he return the interceptions?

4. This former All-American had 163 yards in interception returns and two touchdowns in a season. Name him.

5. What year did he accomplish this?

6. Two players have had 23 tackles for loss in a season. Name them.

Michigan Defense—Questions

7. In what years did they accomplish this?

8. Which player had 174 total tackles in 1977?

9. Which player had tackles totaling 120 yards in losses in a season?

10. What year did he do this?

11. Name the player that had 28 quarterback sacks in three years.

12. Which years did he accomplish this?

13. Two players combined to break up 24 passes in 1982. Name them.

14. Which two players combined for nine fumble recoveries in 1973?

15. Since 1966, three players have had ten career interceptions. Name the last two players and the years they did this.

16. Which player had 202 return yards in interceptions in his career?

17. What years did he play?

18. Name the player who recorded 414 career tackles.

19. What years did he play?

Michigan Defense—Questions

20. Which player had 369 career tackles in 1980-83?

21. Name the player who recorded 326 tackles between 1983 and 1986.

22. Which player recorded 37 tackles for loss in his career?

23. Which years did he do this?

24. Name the player who had 35 career tackles for loss.

25. What years did he play?

26. Mark Messner recorded 26 sacks in his first three years. Who had 19 career sacks?

27. How many sacks did Mike Hammerstein record in his career?

28. How many passes did Dwight Hicks break up in his career?

29. Name the player to record 17 passes broken up in his career.

30. How many fumble recoveries did Mike Hammerstein have in his career?

Michigan Defense (1966-1987) Answers

1. Tom Curtis

2. 1968

3. 182 yards returned

4. Thom Darden

5. 1971

6. Mike Hammerstein and Curtis Greer

7. Hammerstein 1985, Greer 1979

8. Ron Simpkins

9. Mark Messner

Michigan Defense—Answers

10. 1985

11. Mark Messner

12. 1985-1987

13. Marion Body (14) and Jerry Burger (10)

14. Don Dufek (5) and Tom Drake (4)

15. Keith Bostic (1979-1982), Evan Cooper (1980-1983)

16. Dave Brown

17. 1972-1974

18. Paul Girgash

19. 1979-1982

20. Mike Boren

21. Andy Moeller

22. Mike Hammerstein

23. 1981-1985

24. Henry Hill

25. 1968-1970

Michigan Defense—Answers

26. Robert Thompson (1979-1982)

27. 17

28. 18

29. Brad Cochran

30. Seven

University of Michigan Individual Records Questions

1. Who holds the record for the two longest runs from scrimmage?

2. Against which team(s) and in what year(s) did these runs take place?

3. Which quarterbacks hold the record for the two longest passing plays?

4. Who were the receivers?

5. Who were the opponents and what were the years?

6. Who holds the record for the longest punt in UM history?

Individual Records—Questions

7. Against which team did he kick it and in what year?

8. Who holds the record for the longest field goal?

9. Name the opponent and the year it took place.

10. Who holds the record for the longest interception return?

11. Who was the opponent and what was the year?

12. Which player has the longest kickoff return?

13. Name the opponent and the year it took place.

14. Who has recorded the longest punt return?

15. He did it in 1974 against which school?

16. Who led the Wolverines in passing and rushing three years in a row?

17. What years did he do this?

18. Who is the University of Michigan's single season leader in total offense?

19. What was his average per game?

20. Who is the career leader in total offense (average per game)?

Individual Records—Questions

21. What was his career total and average per game?

22. Who was the career leader in total offense (most yards gained)?

23. What was his total and his average per game?

24. Who was the leading quarterback in average yards per completion for a season?

25. What was his average per completion?

26. Name the leading quarterback in average yards per completion for a career.

27. What was his average?

28. Name the two three-time All-Americans from the University of Michigan.

University of Michigan Individual Records Answers

1. Butch Woolfolk

2. Wisconsin in 1979 (92 yards), Wisconsin in 1981 (89 yards)

3. Rick Leach (83 yards) and Jim Harbaugh (77 yards)

4. Leach—Jim Smith, Harbaugh—John Kolesar

5. Leach—Purdue 1975, Harbaugh—Ohio State 1985

6. Monte Robbins

7. Hawaii, 1986

Individual Records—Answers

8. Mike Gillette (53 yards)

9. Iowa, 1986

10. Tom Harmon (95 yards)

11. Iowa, 1939

12. Dennis Fitzgerald (99 yards)

13. Michigan State, 1960

14. Dave Brown (88 yards)

15. Colorado

16. Tom Harmon

17. 1938-1940

18. Jim Harbaugh

19. 219.0 yards per game

20. Jim Harbaugh

21. 5,784 yards, 186.6 yards per game (31 games)

22. Steve Smith (1980-1983)

23. 6,554 yards, 172.5 yards per game (38 games)

24. John Wangler (1979)

Individual Records—Answers

25. 18.3 yards per completion

26. Rick Leach (1975-1978)

27. 17.1 yards per completion

28. Bennie Oosterbaan and Anthony Carter

Team Single Game Records Questions

1. Michigan tallied most net yards in a single game in a 1969 contest. Who was the opponent?

2. How many yards did they gain?

3. Michigan once gave up 515 yards total offense in a game. Who was the opponent?

4. In what season did this occur?

5. In 1979, Michigan set a single game mark of 328 yards passing. Who was the opponent?

6. In which bowl game did this occur?

Team Single Game Records—Questions

7. Name the Wolverine quarterback(s) in that contest.

8. What is the most passing yards a Michigan team has allowed in a single game?

9. Who was the opponent?

10. In what year did this occur?

11. Who won the contest?

12. Name the opponent's quarterback.

13. Michigan has been held to zero net yards passing six times. Who was the last opponent to accomplish this?

14. In what year did they do this?

15. Michigan once held an opponent to minus one net yards passing. Who was the opponent?

16. What year did they do this?

17. Opponents have twice intercepted six Michigan aerials in a single game. Who was the last opponent to do this?

18. What year did this happen?

19. What is the most interceptions Michigan has given up in a game?

Team Single Game Records—Questions

20. Who was the opponent and in what year did this occur?

21. Who was the Michigan quarterback?

22. Michigan has twice attempted 48 passes in a game. What year(s) did this occur?

23. Who were the opponents?

24. The Wolverines once ran 107 plays in a contest. Name the team they did this against.

25. What year did this occur?

26. What was the final score of that contest?

27. In 1951, Michigan was held to six net yards of total offense in a game. Who did this to them?

28. In 1942, Michigan held an opponent to ten net yards total offense. To which team did they do this?

29. What is the most first downs Michigan has made in a game?

30. Who was the opponent and in what year did this occur?

31. Michigan was once held to zero first downs in a contest. Name the opponent.

Team Single Game Records—Questions

32. In what year did this take place?

33. Who won the game?

34. Michigan's highest point total in a game was 130 against West Virginia in 1903. Since 1938, what has been their highest point total?

35. Who was the opponent?

36. Michigan has twice scored 70 points in a contest. Who were the opponents and in what years did this occur?

37. Which team has twice scored 50 points against Michigan?

38. In what years did they do this?

39. Prior to 1988, when was the last time Michigan was held scoreless in a contest?

40. Who was the opponent?

41. When was the last time Michigan has held an opponent scoreless?

42. Who was the opponent?

43. Michigan has twice scored ten touchdowns in Big Ten contests, once in 1975 and again in 1981. Who was the 1975 opponent?

44. What was the final score?

Team Single Game Records—Questions

45. Who was the 1981 opponent?

46. What was the score of that contest?

47. Who was the opponent in Michigan's most decisive loss?

48. What was the score and in what year did this take place?

49. Prior to 1988, which team has twice scored four field goals in a contest against Michigan?

50. In what years did they do this?

51. Who won those contests?

52. When was the last time Michigan played to a 0-0 tie?

53. Who was the opponent?

54. What is the most times Michigan has punted in a game?

55. Who was the opponent?

56. In what year did this occur?

57. How many times did the opponent punt in that same contest?

58. What was the combined yardage on punts in that game?

Team Single Game Records—Questions

59. When was the last time Michigan intercepted six passes in a game?

60. Who was the opponent?

61. What was the final score?

62. What opponent fumbled 12 times in a game against Michigan?

63. In what year did this occur?

64. Michigan once fumbled 12 times in a contest. Name the opponent.

65. In what year did this happen?

66. The Wolverines once recovered eight fumbles in a game. Who was the opponent?

67. What was the final score of that contest?

Team Single Game Records Answers

1. Iowa

2. 673 yards

3. Illinois

4. 1982

5. North Carolina

6. Gator Bowl

7. John Wangler

8. 436 yards

9. Northwestern

Team Single Game Records—Answers

10. 1982

11. Michigan, 49-14

12. Sandy Schwab

13. Ohio State

14. 1976

15. University of Virginia

16. 1971

17. Michigan State

18. 1959

19. Seven

20. Michigan State, 1987

21. Demetrius Brown

22. 1965 and 1966

23. Michigan State both times

24. Minnesota

25. 1968

26. Michigan 33, Minnesota 20

Team Single Game Records—Answers

27. Michigan State
28. Michigan State
29. 37
30. Northwestern, 1978
31. Ohio State
32. 1950
33. Michigan (9-3)
34. 85 points
35. Chicago
36. Navy, 1976 and Illinois, 1981
37. Ohio State
38. 1961 and 1968
39. 1984
40. Iowa
41. 1987
42. Wisconsin
43. Northwestern

Team Single Game Records—Answers

44. 69-0

45. Illinois

46. 70-21

47. Ohio State

48. 50-14, 1968

49. Notre Dame

50. 1979, 1985

51. 1979-Notre Dame, 12-10; 1985-Michigan, 20-12

52. 1938

53. Northwestern

54. 24 times

55. Ohio State

56. 1950

57. 21 times

58. 1,408 yards

59. 1984

Team Single Game Records—Answers

60. Miami (Florida)

61. Michigan 22, Miami 14

62. Wisconsin

63. 1944

64. Illinois

65. 1946

66. Army

67. Michigan 26, Army 2

Team Season Records 1938-1987 Questions

1. In what year did Michigan net a single season high of 5,396 yards total offense?

2. How many of those yards were gained passing?

3. In what year did the Wolverines have their best net yards per game of total offense?

4. What was their average per game that year?

5. How many yards per game rushing did they average that year?

6. How many yards did they average per play that year?

Team Season Records—Questions

7. What year did the Wolverines have their lowest average yards per play?

8. What was their average that year?

9. What year did they rush for 4,144 yards?

10. 1986 was a high-water mark for Michigan in several offensive categories. That year they attempted how many passes?

11. How many passes did they complete?

12. What was their average number of completions per game?

13. What was their completion rate?

14. How many net yards passing per game did they have that year?

15. How many first downs passing did they tally?

16. Michigan scored 644 points in 1902. Since that time, what is their highest scoring season?

17. How many points did they score that year?

18. How many points per game did they average?

19. In what year did they score the fewest points?

20. How many points did they score that year?

Team Season Records—Questions

21. What year did Michigan kick the most field goals in a season?

22. How many did they kick that year?

23. How many did they attempt?

24. When was the last time the Wolverines failed to kick a field goal in a season?

25. How many did they attempt that year?

26. In what year did the Wolverines have their highest net yard per punt average?

27. What was their average that year?

28. Michigan had their most punts returned for touchdown in what year?

29. How many did they have that year?

30. How many times did Michigan fumble in 1950?

31. How many of these did they lose?

32. How many opponents' fumbles did they recover in 1971?

33. What is the most passes Michigan has intercepted in a season?

34. In what year did they do this?

Team Season Records—Questions

35. In what year did they have the most return yards from interceptions?

36. How many yards did they tally?

37. Michigan has twice returned three interceptions for touchdowns in a season. Name the years in which this occurred.

38. Michigan returned how many kickoffs or punts for touchdowns in 1947?

39. Name the year in which Michigan had only 15 return yards on interceptions.

40. In 1945 and 1968, the Wolverines had the fewest fumbles lost for a Wolverine team in a season. How many did they lose?

Team Season Records Answers

1. 1986

2. 2,797

3. 1976

4. 430 yards per game

5. 345.3

6. 6.3 yards per play

7. 1962

8. 2.9 yards per play

9. 1976

Team Season Records—Answers

10. 284
11. 182
12. 14.0 per game
13. .641
14. 215.2 yards per game
15. 119
16. 1976
17. 432 points
18. 36.0 per game
19. 1934
20. 21
21. 1985
22. 20
23. 28
24. 1958
25. Two
26. 1986

Team Season Records—Answers

27. 43.6 yards per punt
28. 1947
29. Four
30. 41 times
31. 23
32. 25
33. 27
34. 1947
35. 1968
36. 447
37. 1947, 1968
38. Seven
39. 1986
40. Five

Big Ten Individual Records (1939-1987)
(Conference games only)
Questions

INDIVIDUAL SINGLE GAME RECORDS

1. Four players have scored 30 points in a single game. Michigan's Ron Johnson did it in 1968. Name the player to accomplish this in 1984.

2. Who was the opponent?

3. Two players have kicked ten PATs in a game. Name the player who did it in a 1981 contest.

4. Who was the opponent?

5. Name the first kicker to make good on five field goals in a game.

47

Big Ten Individual Records—Questions

6. In what year did he accomplish this and who did he play for?

7. Who was the last kicker to do this?

8. In what year did he do it and who did he play for?

9. There have been two 95 yard touchdown passes in the modern era. Name the Purdue quarterback to throw one in the 1955 season.

10. Which quarterback accomplished this in the 1987 season?

11. Who was his receiver on the play?

12. There were two 100-yard pass interceptions for touchdowns in the conference in 1986. Name the defensive backs who accomplished this.

13. Who were the opponents?

14. There have been six 100-yard kickoff returns in the modern era. Who was the last player to accomplish this?

15. In what year did he accomplish this?

16. Who was the opponent?

17. Name the Iowa player who had a 95-yard punt return for a touchdown in 1984.

Big Ten Individual Records—Questions

18. Who was the opponent?

19. Which tailback carried the ball 56 times in a contest in 1987?

20. How many yards did he gain in that game?

21. Who was the oppoennt?

22. Which Michigan State tailback gained 350 yards in one game?

23. Who was the opponent?

24. A Michigan back once gained 347 yards rushing against Purdue. Name him.

25. In what year did he accomplish this?

26. Which school did Mike Adamle play for?

27. What year did he gain 316 yards on 40 carries in a game?

28. Which back averaged 18.0 yards per carry in a 1976 contest?

29. Who did he play for?

30. Which back averaged 17.9 yards per carry in a 1974 contest?

31. Who did he play for?

Big Ten Individual Records—Questions

32. Name the quarterback who had 45 completions in a 1982 game.

33. Who did he play for?

34. Who was the opponent?

35. Which quarterback had 43 completions in a 1980 contest?

36. Who did he play for?

37. Who was the opponent?

38. How many yards did he gain?

39. Which quarterback holds the record for the best completion percentage for a single game (ten or more attempts)?

40. What was his percentage?

41. Who was the opponent?

42. Who holds the conference record for the most consecutive completions?

43. How many did he complete in a row?

44. Who was the opponent?

45. Who holds the record for the most interceptions thrown in a game?

Big Ten Individual Records—Questions

46. How many did he throw?

47. Who was the opponent?

48. Who holds the record for most touchdown passes thrown in a game?

49. How many did he throw?

50. Who was the opponent?

51. Two quarterbacks have thrown six touchdown passes in a game. Who was the last quarterback to do this?

52. Which team did he throw the passes against?

53. Which receiver holds the record for most passes caught in a game?

54. How many did he catch?

55. Who did he play for?

56. Name the team he caught them against.

57. How many yards did he gain?

58. Which wide receiver caught 16 passes in a 1985 game?

59. Who was the opponent?

Big Ten Individual Records—Questions

60. How many touchdowns did he score that day?

61. Which receiver holds the record for most yards gained by passes in a game?

62. How many yards did he gain?

63. Against which team did he do this?

64. Which player caught eight passes totaling 252 yards in a 1983 game?

65. Who did he play for?

66. Who was the opponent?

67. Three players have intercepted four passes in a game. The first two were Clarence Bratt of Wisconsin in 1954 and Paul Beery of Purdue in 1976. Name the third.

68. Which school did he play for and when did he do this?

69. Name the defensive back who had 140 yards in interception returns in a 1970 contest.

70. Who did he play for?

71. Who was the opponent?

72. Two players have caught four touchdown passes in a contest. Name them.

73. Who did they play for?

Big Ten Individual Records—Questions

INDIVIDUAL SEASON RECORDS

74. In the 1980's, which player led the conference in scoring two years in a row?

75. Which years did he do this?

76. How many points did he score each year?

77. How many touchdowns did he score in those two years combined?

78. Which placekicker converted 44 PATs in a season?

79. Who did he play for?

80. Which player led the Big Ten in PATs for two consecutive years in the 1980's?

81. Of those PATs, he converted 42 in 1983. How many did he make in 1984?

82. Who did he play for?

83. Which player led the conference in field goals in 1984?

84. How many did he convert?

85. Who did he play for?

86. Name the Illinois placekicker who led the Big Ten in field goals in 1982.

Big Ten Individual Records—Questions

87. How many did he make?

88. Name the placekicker who made good on 15 field goals out of 17 attempts in 1983.

89. Who did he play for?

90. Which back led the conference in rushing attempts twice in the 1980's with a two year total of 547 carries?

91. Which years did he do this?

92. How many yards did Lorenzo White gain rushing in 1985?

93. Which Michigan back gained 1,155 yards rushing in 1982?

94. Which Big Ten back had the highest average yards per game rushing for a season?

95. What was his average?

96. What year did he accomplish this?

97. Which Big Ten quarterback attempted the most passes in a season?

98. How many did he attempt in his record season?

99. What year did he do this?

100. He also led the conference in passing attempts in 1981. How many did he attempt?

Big Ten Individual Records—Questions

101. In 1982, Tony Eason set the record for most completions in a season. What was his total for the year?

102. Which quarterback completed 215 passes in 1985?

103. Which quarterback has the highest completion percentage for a year?

104. What was his percentage?

105. In what year did he accomplish this?

106. Who had a completion percentage of .672 for the season in 1980?

107. Who did he play for?

108. Name the quarterback that holds the conference record for most yards gained passing in a season.

109. What was his record total?

110. In what year did he do this?

111. Who has the second highest total yards gained passing for a season?

112. What was his total?

113. Who was the second most prolific passer in yards gained in a career?

Big Ten Individual Records—Questions

114. How many touchdown passes did Tony Eason throw in 1981?

115. Three Big Ten quarterbacks have thrown 17 touchdown passes in a season. Name them.

116. Name the quarterback that has the highest passing efficiency rating for a season (minimum 15 attempts per game).

117. What was his rating?

118. Which two quarterbacks have had over 420 plays in total offense in a season?

119. Which quarterback had 5,770 yards rushing and passing in two years?

120. What was his total in 1981?

121. Which player caught 148 passes in two years?

122. Name the player who caught 11 touchdown passes in a season.

123. What year did he do this?

124. What is the record for most pass interceptions in a season?

125. Name the defensive back who accomplished this.

Big Ten Individual Records—Questions

126. In what year did he do this?

127. Name the defensive back who holds the record for most yards returned on interceptions in a season.

128. What was his total?

129. In which year did he accomplish this?

130. Which player holds the record for best punting average in a season?

131. What was his average?

132. Which back holds the record for best punt return average in a season?

133. What was his average?

134. Who holds the record for best kickoff return average for a season?

135. What was his average?

Big Ten Individual Records (1939-1987)
(Conference games only)
Answers

1. Keith Byars (Ohio State)

2. Illinois

3. Ali-Haji Shiekh (Michigan)

4. Illinois

5. Dan Beaver

6. 1973, Illinois

7. Chris White

8. 1984, Illinois

9. Len Dawson

Big Ten Individual Records—Answers

10. Chuck Hartleib (Iowa)

11. Quinn Early

12. David Brown (Ohio State), Rod Woodson (Purdue)

13. Brown-Purdue, Woodson-Iowa

14. Michael Jones (Wisconsin)

15. 1984

16. Northwestern

17. Bill Happel

18. Minnesota

19. Lorenzo White

20. 292 yards

21. Indiana

22. Eric Allen (1971)

23. Purdue

24. Ron Johnson

25. 1968

Big Ten Individual Records—Answers

26. Northwestern

27. 1969

28. Rob Lytle (ten carries for 180 yards)

29. Michigan

30. Mike Pruitt (ten carries for 179 yards)

31. Purdue

32. Sandy Schwab (71 attempts)

33. Northwestern

34. Michigan

35. Dave Wilson (69 attempts)

36. Illinois

37. Ohio State

38. 621

39. Jim Harbaugh

40. .923 (12 of 13)

41. Purdue (1985)

Big Ten Individual Records—Answers

42. Chuck Long

43. 22

44. Indiana

45. Demetrius Brown

46. Seven

47. Michigan State (1987)

48. Chuck Hartleib

49. Seven

50. Northwestern

51. Chuck Long (Iowa)

52. Northwestern

53. Jon Harvey

54. 17

55. Northwestern

56. Michigan

57. 208 yards

58. David Williams (Illinois)

Big Ten Individual Records—Answers

59. Purdue (1985)

60. Three

61. Quinn Early

62. 256 (ten catches)

63. Northwestern (1987)

64. Al Toon

65. Wisconsin

66. Purdue

67. John Miller

68. Michigan State, 1987

69. Walt Bowser

70. Minnesota

71. Michigan State

72. Reggie Arnold (1977) and Quinn Early (1987)

73. Arnold-Purdue, Early-Iowa

74. Keith Byars

75. 1983, 1984

Big Ten Individual Records—Answers

76. 1983-114; 1984-120

77. 39

78. Morten Anderson

79. Michigan State

80. Rich Spangler

81. 39

82. Ohio State

83. Chris White

84. 19

85. Illinois

86. Mike Bass

87. 18

88. Bob Bergeron

89. Michigan

90. Lorenzo White

91. 1985, 1987

92. 1,470

Big Ten Individual Records—Answers

93. Lawrence Ricks

94. Lorenzo White

95. 183.7 yards a game

96. 1985

97. Tony Eason (Illinois)

98. 354

99. 1982

100. 349

101. 222

102. Jack Trudeau

103. Chuck Long

104. .673

105. 1984

106. Mark Hermann

107. Purdue

108. Tony Eason

109. 3,024 yards

Big Ten Individual Records—Answers

110. 1981

111. Tony Eason (1982)

112. 2,680

113. Jim Everett (4,995 yards in 1984 and 1985)

114. 20

115. Dave Wilson, Randy Wright and Chuck Hartleib

116. Jim Harbaugh

117. 178.5

118. Tony Eason (428) and Sandy Schwab (425)

119. Tony Eason (1981-1982)

120. 3,008

121. David Williams (1984-1985)

122. Anthony Carter

123. 1980

124. Nine

125. Tom Curtis (Michigan)

126. 1968

Big Ten Individual Records—Answers

127. Walt Bowser

128. 203 yards

129. 1970

130. Greg Montgomery

131. 49.7 yards per punt

132. Dean Look (Michigan State University)

133. 32.5 return yards per punt (1958)

134. Stan Brown (Purdue)

135. 41.1 yards per kickoff (1970)

Big Ten Team Records (1939-1987)
(Conference games only)
Questions

TEAM SINGLE GAME RECORDS

1. Which team holds the record for most points scored in a game?

2. How many points did they score?

3. Who was the opponent?

4. Which team scored 83 points in a 1950 game?

5. Who was the opponent?

6. Four different teams have scored two safeties in a game. Name the last team to do this.

Big Ten Team Records—Questions

7. Who was the opponent?

8. Which team once scored 11 points after touchdowns in a game?

9. Which team has twice converted ten points after touchdowns in a game?

10. When was the last time they did this?

11. Who was the opponent?

12. Which team has converted five field goals in a game on three different occasions?

13. When was the last time they did this?

14. Which team holds the record for most rushes in a contest?

15. How many times did they rush?

16. Who was the opponent?

17. Which team holds the record for fewest rushes in a game?

18. How many times did they rush?

19. Name their opponent in that game.

20. Two teams share the record for most yards rushing in a game. Name them.

Big Ten Team Records—Questions

21. What were their individual totals?

22. Who were their opponents?

23. Which team holds the record for fewest yards gained rushing in a game?

24. What was their total?

25. Who was their opponent?

26. Which team holds the record for the most passes thrown in a game?

27. Did they win the game?

28. Who was their opponent?

29. Which team holds the record for fewest pass attempts in a game?

30. How many did they attempt and against which team?

31. What team holds the record for most passes completed in a game?

32. How many did they complete?

33. What was the last team to have zero pass completions in a game?

34. How many did they attempt and who was their opponent?

Big Ten Team Records—Questions

35. The most yards gained passing in a game is 621. Which team accomplished this?

36. Name their opponent in that contest.

37. Which team holds the record for best completion average in a game?

38. What was their average?

39. Which team has the best completion average for a game (more than eight attempts)?

40. What was their average?

41. Who was their opponent?

42. What team has the most touchdown passes in a game?

43. How many did they have?

44. What team has run the most plays (passing and rushing) in a game?

45. How many plays did they run?

46. Name their opponent in that contest.

47. Which team holds the record for fewest plays in a contest?

48. How many plays did they have?

Big Ten Team Records—Questions

49. Which team has most total offense in a game?

50. How many yards did they gain?

51. Who was their opponent?

52. What is the highest total offense Michigan has had in a game?

53. Name their opponent in that game.

54. What was the final score?

55. Which team has fewest yards gained in a game?

56. What was their total?

57. Which team holds the record for most fumbles in a game?

58. How many times did they fumble?

59. How many of those did they lose?

60. Which team has lost the most fumbles in a game?

61. How many did they lose?

62. Who was their opponent?

Big Ten Team Records—Questions

TEAM SEASON RECORDS

63. Name the team that holds the record for most points per game in a season.

64. What was their average?

65. What year did they accomplish this?

66. Which team had fewest points per game (minimum five games)?

67. How many points per game did they average?

68. In 1939, Chicago scored zero points in three conference games. How many points did they allow that year?

69. Which team allowed 47.2 points per game in 1981?

70. Which team allowed 46.3 points per game in 1983?

71. Name the team that allowed fewest points per game for a season.

72. How many did they allow per game?

73. Which team averaged 69.5 rushes per game in 1973?

74. Which team averaged 365.1 yards gained rushing in one year?

Big Ten Team Records—Questions

75. Name the team that holds the record for fewest yards allowed rushing per game for a season.

76. What was their average?

77. Which team attempted the most passes per game for a season?

78. How many did they attempt per game?

79. Name the team that completed the most passes per game in a season.

80. How many did they complete per game?

81. Which team had fewest pass attempts per game for a season?

82. How many did they attempt per contest?

83. Which team had fewest pass completions per game in a season?

84. How many did they complete per game?

85. Which team had most yards gained passing per game for a season?

86. What was their average per game?

87. Name the team that averaged the most yards per game total offense for a season.

Big Ten Team Records—Questions

88. What was their average per game?

89. Which team allowed the least yards per game total offense for a season?

90. Which team averaged the fewest fumbles per game for a season?

91. How many fumbles did they average per game?

Big Ten Team Records (1939-1987)
(Conference games only)
Answers

TEAM SINGLE GAME RECORDS

1. Michigan

2. 85

3. Chicago

4. Ohio State

5. Iowa

6. Minnesota (1981)

7. Indiana

8. Ohio State (1950 against Iowa)

77

Big Ten Team Records—Answers

9. Michigan

10. 1981

11. Illinois

12. Illinois

13. 1984 (against Minnesota)

14. Purdue

15. 92 (483 yards)

16. Iowa (1968)

17. Purdue

18. 14 (−18 yards)

19. MSU (1987)

20. Michigan and Michigan State

21. 573 yards

22. Michigan-Northwestern (1975), Michigan State-Purdue (1971)

23. Iowa (1941)

24. −87 yards

Big Ten Team Records—Answers

25. Wisconsin

26. Northwestern (1982)

27. No

28. Michigan

29. Minnesota (1940)

30. Zero, Ohio State

31. Northwestern (1982)

32. 45 (against Michigan)

33. Minnesota (1985)

34. Seven, Indiana

35. Illinois (1980)

36. Ohio State

37. Ohio State

38. 1.000 (8-8) against Iowa in 1975

39. Michigan (1985)

40. .923 (12-13, 230 yards)

41. Purdue

Big Ten Team Records—Answers

42. Iowa (1987)

43. Seven (against Northwestern)

44. Indiana (1978)

45. 109 (68 rushes, 41 passes)

46. Minnesota

47. Iowa (1944)

48. 34 (31 rush, 3 pass)

49. Iowa (1983)

50. 713

51. Northwestern

52. 673 yards (1969)

53. Iowa

54. Michigan 51, Iowa 6

55. Iowa (1941)

56. −19 (−87 rush, 68 pass)

57. Michigan State (1971)

58. 14

Big Ten Team Records—Answers

59. Three

60. Illinois (twice-1948 and 1987)

61. Eight

62. 1948-Wisconsin, 1987-Purdue

TEAM SEASON RECORDS

63. Michigan State

64. 41.0 points per game

65. 1978

66. Illinois (1941)

67. 2.6 points per game

68. 192 (64.0 average)

69. Northwestern

70. Minnesota

71. Illinois (1951)

72. 3.8 points per game

73. Ohio State

Big Ten Team Records—Answers

74. Ohio State (1973)

75. Michigan State (1965)

76. 34.6 yards per game

77. Illinois (1980)

78. 43.9 per game

79. Illinois (1985)

80. 27.6 per game

81. Minnesota (1943)

82. 4.0 attempts per game

83. Minnesota (twice, 1940 and 1943)

84. 1.0 per game

85. Illinois (1985)

86. 340.2 yards per game

87. Michigan State (1978)

88. 523.1 yards per game

89. Michigan (1943)

90. Purdue (1975) and Minnesota (1976)

91. 1.0 per game

More Big Ten Trivia Questions

1. Match the Big Ten school with the stadium its football team uses for home games:

   a) Illinois
   b) Indiana
   c) Iowa
   d) Michigan
   e) Michigan State
   f) Minnesota
   g) Northwestern
   h) Ohio State
   i) Purdue
   j) Wisconsin

   Ross-Ade Stadium
   Dyche Stadium
   Kinnick Stadium
   Hubert H. Humphrey Metrodome
   Memorial Stadium (52,354 seats)
   Camp Randall Stadium
   _____ Stadium (85,339 seats)
   Memorial Stadium (69,200 seats)
   _____ Stadium (76,000 seats)
   _____ Stadium (101,701 seats)

More Big Ten Trivia—Questions

2. Fill in the school each Head Coach represents:

   a) John Mackovic   f) John Cooper
   b) Francis Peay   g) Hayden Fry
   c) Fred Akers   h) John Gutekunst
   d) Bo Schembechler i) Don Morton
   e) Bill Mallory   j) George Perles

3. What was the largest single game attendance in Big Ten history?

4. Where did this take place?

5. Who was the visiting team and what was the date?

6. Who won the game?

7. Which former University of Michigan player became President of the United States?

8. Which Big Ten quarterback holds the record for most yards gained in a single game?

9. Who did he play for?

10. Who was the opponent and what was the date?

11. How many yards did he gain?

12. Which Big Ten quarterback threw seven touchdown passes against Northwestern in 1987?

More Big Ten Trivia—Questions

13. Which receiver caught four of those passes?

14. How many passes did the above receiver catch in that game?

15. Which former tight end caught 17 passes in a single game?

16. How many yards did he gain with his 17 catches?

17. Who did he play for?

18. Who was the opponent?

19. Which former tailback scored 20 touchdowns in 1984?

20. What player gained 1,470 yards in 1985?

21. Who did he play for?

22. How many yards did he average per game?

23. Which quarterback attempted 354 passes in 1982?

24. How many did he complete?

25. Who did he play for?

26. Which former Purdue quarterback gained 2,545 yards in a season?

More Big Ten Trivia—Questions

27. Which year did he do this?

28. Which two quarterbacks each threw 16 touchdown passes in 1985?

29. Which quarterback holds the conference record for highest passing efficiency for a season (minimum 15 attempts per game)?

30. What was his efficiency rating and in what year did he accomplish this rating?

31. Which quarterback completed 215 passes in 1985?

32. Which team did he play for?

33. Which quarterback completed 199 passes in 1982?

34. Who did he play for?

35. Name the receiver who caught 11 touchdown passes in 1980.

36. Who did he play for?

37. Which defensive back grabbed nine interceptions in 1968?

38. Who did he play for?

39. How many return yards did his interceptions net?

More Big Ten Trivia—Questions

40. What player led the conference in most passes caught in 1984?

41. Who did he play for?

42. How many passes did he catch that year?

43. In 1981, quarterback Tony Eason gained 3,024 yards passing. How many yards of total offense did he have that year?

44. Which punter led the conference in punting average in 1986?

45. What was his average?

46. Who did he play for?

47. Which halfback led the conference in best average and most touchdowns on kickoff returns in 1970?

48. How many did he return for touchdowns?

49. What was his average yards per return for the year?

50. Who did he play for?

More Big Ten Trivia Answers

1. MATCH THE STADIUMS

   a) Memorial Stadium (69, 200)
   b) Memorial Stadium (52, 354)
   c) Kinnick Stadium
   d) Michigan Stadium (101, 701)
   e) Spartan Stadium
   f) Hubert H. Humphrey Metrodome
   g) Dyche Stadium
   h) Ohio Stadium (85, 339)
   i) Ross-Ade Stadium
   j) Camp Randall Stadium

2. a) Mackovic-Illinois
   b) Peay-Northwestern
   c) Akers-Purdue
   d) Schembechler-Michigan

More Big Ten Trivia—Answers

      e) Mallory-Indiana
      f) Cooper-Ohio State
      g) Fry-Iowa
      h) Gutekunst-Minnesota
      i) Morton-Wisconsin
      j) Perles-Michigan State

3. 106,255

4. Michigan Stadium (Ann Arbor)

5. Ohio State, November 17, 1979

6. Ohio State, 18-15

7. Gerald Ford

8. Dave Wilson

9. Illinois

10. Ohio State, November 8, 1980

11. 585 (43 of 69 for 621 passing, 7 rushes for minus 36 yards)

12. Chuck Hartleib (Iowa)

13. Quinn Early

14. Ten for 256 yards

15. Jon Harvey

More Big Ten Trivia—Answers

16. 208 yards
17. Northwestern
18. Michigan, October 23, 1982
19. Keith Byars
20. Lorenzo White
21. Michigan State
22. 183.7
23. Tony Eason
24. 222
25. Illinois
26. Jim Everett
27. 1985
28. Jim Harbaugh and Chuck Long
29. Jim Harbaugh
30. 178.5, 1985
31. Jack Trudeau
32. Illinois

More Big Ten Trivia—Answers

33. Sandy Schwab

34. Northwestern

35. Anthony Carter

36. Michigan

37. Tom Curtis

38. Michigan

39. 182

40. David Williams

41. Illinois

42. 85

43. 3,008 (minus 16 yards rushing)

44. Greg Montgomery

45. 49.7 yards per punt

46. Michigan State

47. Stan Brown

48. 3 (100, 96, and 93 yards)

49. 41.1 yards per return

50. Purdue

Big Ten Coaches Questions

1. Name the former Michigan coach who was an All-American in football and basketball and who led the Big Ten in baseball hitting.

2. Which coach created the distinctive winged-helmet that is still worn by Michigan teams?

3. Name the coach who led the Wolverines to the national championship in his first year as head coach.

4. What coach led Michigan to the national championship in his last year at the helm?

5. Name the coach credited with founding the "two-platoon" system.

Big Ten Coaches—Questions

6. Who was the opponent in Coach Schembechler's first Michigan win?

7. Which active NCAA 1-A coach has the most career wins?

8. Which former Big Ten coach had more wins than Bo?

9. Name the three other former coaches with more wins (nationally).

10. What team did the Wolverines defeat for Bo's 166th 'M' win (school record)?

11. Where did John Mackovic coach before coming to Illinois?

12. Which Big Eight school did Bill Mallory coach at?

13. At which two schools did Hayden Fry coach before joining Iowa?

14. Name the school Bo Schembechler was head coach at before he came to Michigan.

15. Which Western Athletic Conference school did Fred Akers coach at?

Big Ten Coaches Answers

1. Bennie Oosterbaan

2. Fritz Crisler

3. Bennie Oosterbaan

4. Fritz Crisler

5. Fritz Crisler

6. Vanderbilt

7. Bo Schembechler

8. Woody Hayes

9. Bear Bryant, Amos Alonzo Stagg, Pop Warner

Big Ten Coaches—Answers

10. Ohio State (November 22, 1986)

11. Wake Forest (1978-1980)

12. Colorado (1974-1978)

13. Southern Methodist (1962-1972), North Texas State (1973-1978)

14. Miami (Ohio), 1963-1968

15. Wyoming (1975-1976)

Michigan vs. The Big Ten and Others—Who Dunit? Questions

1. Which Michigan player caught eight passes against Wisconsin in 1986?

2. This Wolverine had nine receptions in a game in 1980. Name him.

3. Who was the opponent?

4. Which University of Michigan receiver caught ten passes against Purdue in a single game?

5. What year did he do this?

6. Name the Michigan player who caught a 62 yard pass in 1987.

Michigan vs. Big Ten and Others—Questions

7. Who was the opponent?

8. Which Wolverine caught a 77 yard touchdown pass in 1985?

9. Against which team did he do this?

10. In 1975, Jim Smith caught an 83 yard touchdown pass. Against which team did he do this?

11. Michigan gained 546 total yards against which team in 1987?

12. Michigan gained 604 total yards against who in 1985?

13. How many first downs did the Wolverines have in that game?

14. Jamie Morris once gained 234 yards rushing in a contest. Who was the opponent?

15. What year did he do this?

16. Has Michigan ever had less than 25 rushing attempts in a game?

17. Against who did Michigan gain 531 yards rushing in 1976?

18. Michigan held an opponent to −13 yards rushing in 1987. Name the opponent.

Michigan vs. Big Ten and Others—Questions

19. Which back had a 98 yard run from scrimmage against the Wolverines in 1987?

20. What team did he play for?

21. Jamie Morris had a 77 yard touchdown run against what team in a bowl game?

22. In 1979, which Michigan back had a 92 yard touchdown run against Wisconsin?

23. This same back had a long touchdown run against Wisconsin in 1981. How long was it?

24. How many passes did Dick Vidmer attempt against Michigan State in 1966?

25. Which Wolverine completed 21 passes against Purdue in 1984?

26. Which opposing quarterback passed for 362 yards against Michigan in 1987?

27. Which quarterback did Michigan intercept five times in a 1985 game?

28. Who did he play for?

29. Which quarterback did the Wolverines intercept six times in 1984?

30. How many touchdown passes did Chris Zurbrugg throw against Purdue in 1984?

Michigan vs. Big Ten and Others—Questions

31. In 1987 how many passes did Michigan complete against Northwestern?

32. Which opponent did Michigan hold to two completions in 1987?

33. Which opponent did not punt against Michigan in 1986?

34. This Michigan player kicked a 71-yard punt in 1987. Name him.

35. Who was the opponent?

36. Which player had a 86-yard punt against Michigan in 1986?

37. Who did he play for?

38. Name the Wolverine who booted a 82-yard punt against Hawaii.

39. What year did he do this?

40. Which Michigan player intercepted three passes in a 1986 contest?

41. Who was the opponent?

42. Which Michigan State player intercepted four Michigan passes in 1987?

43. Which opposing team turned the ball over seven times against Michigan in 1985?

Michigan vs. Big Ten and Others—Questions

44. Michigan lost five fumbles against which opponent in 1985?

45. Which Ohio State back scored three touchdowns in the 1984 Michigan—OSU contest?

46. This Ohio State back scored four touchdowns against the Wolverines in 1968. Name him.

47. Which Michigan player scored five touchdowns against Wisconsin in 1968?

48. This Big Ten player kicked four field goals against Michigan in 1985. Name him.

49. Who did he play for?

50. Which Wolverine returned a kickoff 73 yards for a touchdown in 1972?

51. Who was the opponent?

52. Name the Michigan player who ran a punt back 85 yards for a touchdown in 1985.

53. Name the opponent.

54. Which Michigan State player returned a punt 87 yards for a touchdown against Michigan in 1984?

55. In the 1985 Michigan—Michigan State contest, Wolverine Ed Hood returned a blocked punt for a touchdown. Who blocked the punt?

Michigan vs. Big Ten and Others—Questions

56. In 1985, Michigan scored a safety against which opponent?

57. The Wolverines scored 31 points in one quarter against which 1983 opponent?

58. Michigan scored 42 points in one half against which 1987 opponent?

59. In 1986, Wolverine placekicker Mike Gillette kicked a 52-yard field goal against which opponent?

60. Name the team that scored 42 points against Michigan in 1958.

Michigan vs. The Big Ten and Others—Who Dunit? Answers

1. Ken Higgins

2. Anthony Carter

3. Minnesota

4. Jim Mandich

5. 1969

6. Greg McMurtry

7. Minnesota

8. John Kolesar

9. Ohio State

Michigan vs. The Big Ten and Others—Answers

10. Purdue

11. Long Beach State

12. Indiana

13. 30

14. Alabama

15. 1988 (Hall of Fame Bowl)

16. No

17. Stanford

18. Iowa

19. Darrell Thompson

20. Minnesota

21. Alabama in the 1988 Hall of Fame Bowl

22. Butch Woolfolk

23. 89 yards

24. 47 passes

25. Chris Zurbrugg

26. Chuck Hartleib (Iowa)

Michigan vs. Big Ten and Others—Answers

27. Mike Howard

28. Wisconsin

29. Bernie Kosar

30. Four

31. One

32. Wisconsin

33. Notre Dame

34. Monte Robbins

35. Minnesota

36. Greg Montgomery

37. Michigan State

38. Monte Robbins

39. 1987

40. Andy Moeller

41. Wisconsin

42. John Miller

43. Wisconsin

Michigan vs. Big Ten and Others—Answers

44. North Carolina

45. Keith Byars

46. James Otis

47. Ron Johnson

48. Rob Houghtlin

49. Iowa

50. Gil Chapman

51. Illinois

52. Gilvanni Johnson

53. Minnesota

54. Bobby Morse

55. Dieter Heren

56. Purdue

57. Minnesota

58. Wisconsin

59. Illinois

60. Northwestern

Photographs Questions

1. Name the Michigan ball carrier, the opposing team, and number 32 in the white jersey.

Photographs—Questions

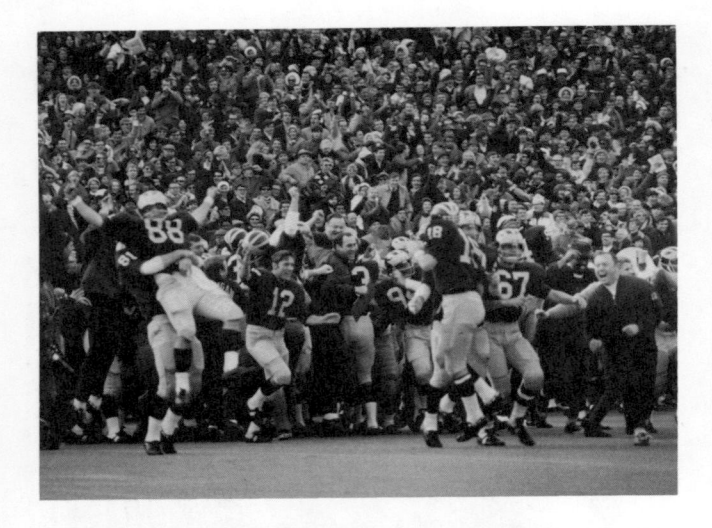

2. This celebration took place in 1969. What was the occasion and who is number 18?

Photographs—Questions

3. Number 48 scored two touchdowns in this 1969 game against OSU. Name him, and numbers 42 and 72.

Photographs—Questions

4. This player was team captain in 1969. Name him.

Photographs—Questions

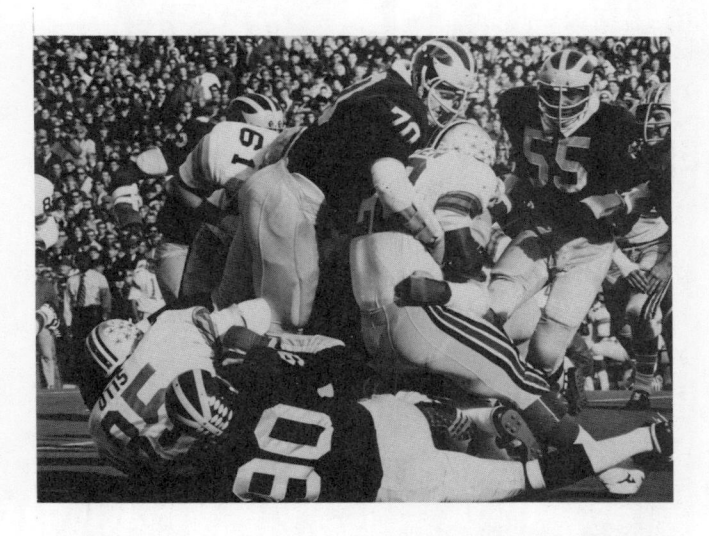

5. In this 1969 contest, name the three University of Michigan players surrounding the ball carrier.

111

Photographs—Questions

6. Name the player and the coach.

Photographs—Questions

7. Name the ball carrier Leach is handing off to and the opposing team.

Photographs—Questions

8. In this 1979 game, name the ball carrier and the opponent.

114

Photographs—Questions

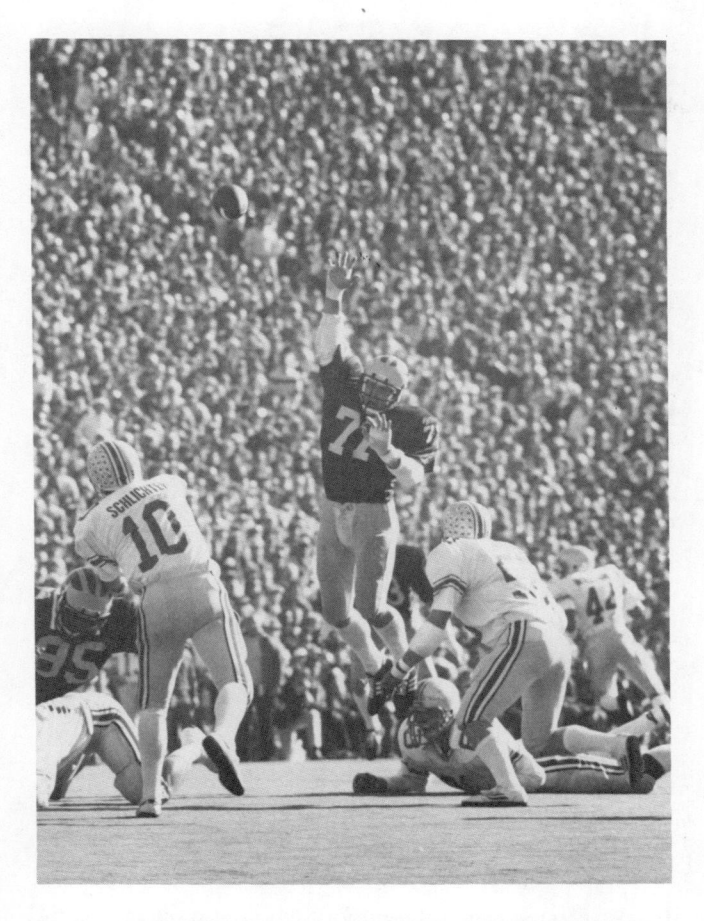

9. Who is attempting to block this Art Schlichter pass?

Photographs—Questions

10. Name the University of Michigan player tackling the ball carrier.

Photographs—Questions

11. In this 1979 contest, who is the ball carrier and who is the opponent?

117

Photographs—Questions

12. In this 1979 contest, name the opponent's quarterback (number 14) and the Wolverine breaking up the pass.

Photographs—Questions

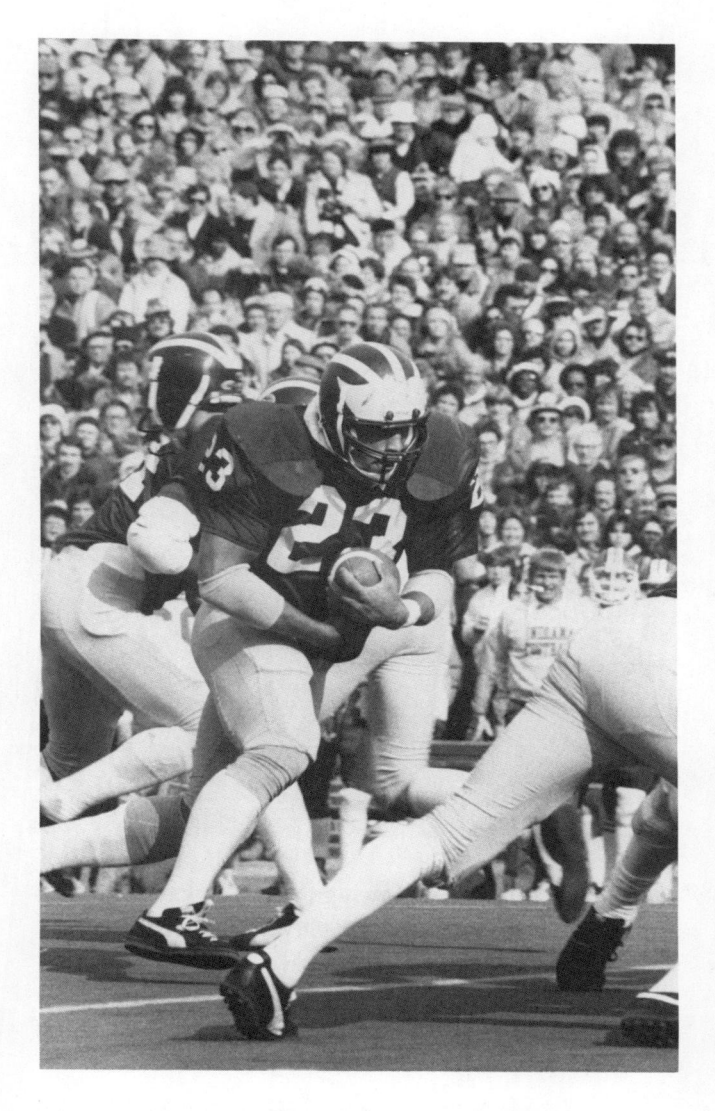

13. Name this former Michigan fullback.

Photographs—Questions

14. In this shot following the 1979 victory over Indiana, identify this player.

Photographs—Questions

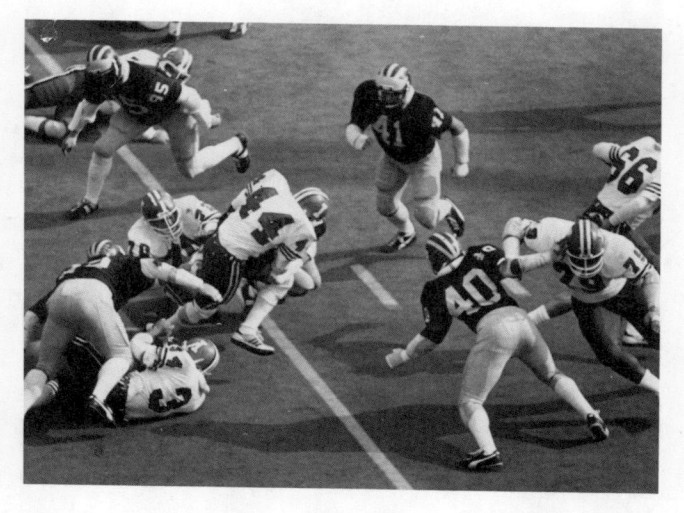

15. Andy Cannavino (number 41) and Ron Simpkins (number 40) zero in on number 44. Identify him.

Photographs—Questions

16. Who is Michigan's number 53 (with hand on the ball carrier's ankle)?

Photographs—Questions

17.   Identify this University of Michigan kicker.

Photographs—Questions

18. Name the ball carrier and opponent.

124

Photographs—Questions

19. Name this former University of Michigan great.

125

Photographs—Questions

20. Name the ball carrier and the opposing team.

Photographs—Questions

21. Stan Edwards goes for the ball in this 1980 game. Name the opposing team.

Photographs Answers

1. Glen Doughty, Ohio State, Jack Tatum

2. Victory over Ohio State, John Gabler

3. Garvie Craw (48), Billy Taylor (42) and Dan Dierdorf (72)

4. Jim Mandich

5. Mike Keller (90), Marty Huff (70), Cecil Pryor (55)

6. Rick Leach, Bo Schembechler

7. Russell Davis, Purdue

Photographs—Answers

8. John Wangler, Ohio State

9. Mike Trgovac

10. Ron Simpkins

11. Curtis Greer, Minnesota

12. Tim Clifford (Indiana), Andy Cannavino

13. Lawrence Reid (against Indiana in 1979)

14. Ali-Haji-Sheikh

15. Lonnie Johnson (Indiana)

16. Mel Owens

17. Don Bracken

18. Butch Woolfolk, South Carolina

19. Anthony Carter

20. Butch Woolfolk, Michigan State

21. Notre Dame

Michigan in The Bowl Games Questions

1. What year did Michigan first play in the Rose Bowl?

2. Who did they play?

3. What was the final score?

4. Where was the game played?

5. What was the attendance?

6. Who was the Michigan coach?

7. Due to the lopsided score of the first Rose Bowl game, the following year the football game was replaced by what kind of contest?

Michigan in The Bowl Games—Questions

8. When did the Wolverines play in their next bowl game?

9. Which bowl game did they play in?

10. Who did they play?

11. Who won the game?

12. In the 1947 season leading up to the 1948 Rose Bowl victory, which two University of Michigan backs won All-America honors?

13. Quarterback Bob Chappius finished second in the Heisman Trophy balloting in 1947. Who finished first?

14. Who was the Michigan head coach in 1947?

15. When was Michigan's next Rose Bowl appearance?

16. Who was the opponent?

17. In the Michigan locker room at half time and trailing 6-0, who said, "Victory is still ours"?

18. What was the final score of the game?

19. Who was the Wolverine's next Rose Bowl opponent?

20. In what year did the contest take place?

Michigan in The Bowl Games—Questions

21. Which University of Michigan player ran 84 yards for a touchdown in that game?

22. Who was the Michigan quarterback?

23. What was the final score?

24. Michigan returned to the Rose Bowl again in 1970. Who did they play against?

25. Who won the game?

26. Who was Michigan's Head Coach?

27. What happened to him the night before the game?

28. Who assumed the coaching responsibilities for the game?

29. Who was USC's head coach?

30. After another trip to the Rose Bowl in 1972, Michigan's next bowl appearance was on January 1, 1976. What bowl game did they appear in?

31. Who was their opponent?

32. What was the significance of that bowl appearance?

33. What was the score of the contest?

Michigan in The Bowl Games—Questions

34. Who was Michigan's quarterback?

35. Michigan's opponent was led on defense by two brothers. Name them.

36. The Wolverine team that went to the Rose Bowl in 1977 led the nation in three major categories. Which categories were they?

37. Who won the game?

38. That contest was the last game for a University of Michigan back who gained a career total of 3,317 yards. Name him.

39. Which opponent did the Wolverines face in the 1978 Rose Bowl?

40. Michigan scored 20 points in the second half. Who won the game?

41. What was the final score?

42. In 1979, Michigan returned to the Rose Bowl again. Who was their opponent?

43. Who won the game?

44. What controversial play marred the game?

45. Which bowl game did the Wolverines appear in on December 28, 1979?

46. Who was their opponent?

Michigan in The Bowl Games—Questions

47. What was the score?

48. Which Michigan player caught four passes for 141 yards and two touchdowns in that game?

49. On January 1, 1981, Michigan played Washington in the Rose Bowl. What was the significance of that game for Bo?

50. What was the final score?

51. Which Wolverine back gained 182 yards in that contest?

52. Who was the Michigan placekicker in that game?

53. Who won game MVP honors?

54. On December 31, 1981, Michigan played in what bowl game?

55. In what city was the contest?

56. Who was Michigan's opponent?

57. What was the final score?

58. In that contest, Haji-Sheikh connected on the longest field goal of his college career. How long was it?

59. Who was the University of Michigan quarterback?

Michigan in The Bowl Games—Questions

60. How many yards did UCLA gain on the ground?

61. Who was Michigan's opponent in the 1983 Rose Bowl?

62. What was the final score?

63. What type of injury forced University of Michigan quarterback Steve Smith from the game in the second quarter?

64. Who was his replacement?

65. What bowl game did the Wolverines play in on January 1, 1984?

66. Who was the opponent?

67. What was the final score?

68. Which opponent back ran for 130 yards?

69. Which bowl game did Michigan appear in on December 21, 1984?

70. Name the city it was played in.

71. Who was the opponent?

72. Which conference did the opponent represent?

73. What was the final score?

Michigan in The Bowl Games—Questions

74. What was the significance of the game for the winners?

75. Who was the opponent's quarterback?

76. What was the next bowl game Michigan played in?

77. Who was the opponent?

78. What city was the game played in?

79. What was the score at half time?

80. Who won the game?

81. Which back ran for 156 yards in that contest?

82. In the 1987 Rose Bowl, Michigan's opponent made their first appearance in that particular bowl game. Name the opponent.

83. Who won the game?

Michigan in The Bowl Games Answers

1. 1902, the inaugural Rose Bowl game

2. Stanford

3. Michigan 49, Stanford 0

4. Tournament Park—Pasadena, California

5. 8,000

6. Fielding H. Yost

7. Chariot Race

8. 1948

9. Rose Bowl

Michigan in The Bowl Games—Answers

10. Southern California

11. Michigan, 49-0

12. Quarterback Bob Chappuis and halfback Bump Elliot

13. Johnny Lujack

14. Fritz Crisler

15. 1951

16. California Golden Bears (Berkley)

17. Head Coach Bennie Oosterbaan

18. Michigan 14, California 6

19. Oregon State

20. 1965

21. Mel Anthony

22. Bob Timberlake

23. Michigan 34, Oregon State 7

24. Southern California

25. Southern California, 10-3

Michigan in The Bowl Games—Answers

26. Bo Schembechler

27. He suffered a heart attack.

28. Defensive coordinator Jim Young

29. John McKay

30. Orange Bowl

31. Oklahoma

32. It was the first year Big Ten teams were allowed to appear in post-season bowl games other than the Rose Bowl.

33. Oklahoma 14, Michigan 6

34. Rick Leach

35. Leroy and Dewey Selmon

36. Total offense (448.1 yards per game), scoring offense (38.7 points per game) and scoring defense (7.2 points per game)

37. USC, 14-6

38. Rob Lytle

39. Washington Huskies

Michigan in The Bowl Games—Answers

40. Washington

41. 27-20

42. Southern California

43. USC (17-10)

44. USC tailback Charles White fumbled at the goal line but the line judge ruled that he had scored.

45. Gator Bowl

46. North Carolina

47. UNC 17, Michigan 15

48. Anthony Carter

49. It was his first Rose Bowl win in six tries.

50. Michigan 23, Washington 6

51. Butch Woolfolk

52. Ali-Haji-Sheikh

53. Butch Woolfolk

54. Bluebonnet Bowl

55. Houston, Texas

Michigan in The Bowl Games—Answers

56. UCLA

57. Michigan 33, UCLA 14

58. 47 yards

59. Steve Smith

60. 33 yards

61. UCLA

62. UCLA 24, Michigan 14

63. Separated shoulder

64. Dave Hall

65. Sugar Bowl

66. Auburn

67. Auburn 9, Michigan 7

68. Bo Jackson

69. Holiday Bowl

70. San Diego, California

71. BYU

72. WAC (Western Athletic Conference)

Michigan in The Bowl Games—Answers

73. BYU 24, Michigan 17

74. It clinched the National Championship for BYU.

75. Robbie Bosco

76. Fiesta Bowl (January 1, 1986)

77. Nebraska

78. Tempe, Arizona

79. Nebraska 14, Michigan 3

80. Michigan (27-23)

81. Jamie Morris

82. Arizona State University

83. ASU (22-15)

Wolverines in The Pro Draft (1937-1987) Questions

1. Who was the first Michigan player to be picked in the first round of the NFL draft?

2. Which team drafted him and in what year?

3. What other Michigan player was also picked in the first round that year?

4. Which team picked him?

5. Name the player picked in the first round in 1942.

6. Which team picked him?

Wolverines in The Pro Draft—Questions

7. Elroy Hirsch was picked in the first round in the 1945 draft by Cleveland. Which other Wolverine was picked in round number one that year and which team picked him?

8. Michigan has twice had ten players picked in the NFL draft. Which years did this happen?

9. In the 1972 draft, which University of Michigan defensive back was picked in the first round?

10. Which team picked him?

11. In the same draft, which Michigan guard was picked in the second round?

12. The guard referred to in the previous question became an important blocker for which famous pro back?

13. In the 1975 pro draft, which Wolverine was picked in the first round?

14. Name the team that picked him.

15. Which University of Michigan running back was picked by the Denver Broncos in the 1977 draft?

16. Which round was he picked in?

Wolverines in The Pro Draft—Questions

17. In the 1980 draft, this player was the sixth pick overall. Name him.

18. Which team picked him?

19. Who was the last Wolverine to be picked in the first round?

20. Who was the only University of Michigan player picked in the 1985 draft?

21. What round was he picked in?

Wolverines in The Pro Draft (1937-1987) Answers

1. Tom Harmon

2. Chicago Bears, 1941

3. Forest Evashevski

4. Washington

5. Bob Westfall

6. Detroit Lions

7. Don Lund, Chicago Bears

8. 1972 and 1974

9. Thom Darden

Wolverines in The Pro Draft—Answers

10. Cleveland Browns

11. Reggie McKenzie

12. O.J. Simpson

13. Defensive Back Dave Brown

14. Pittsburgh Steelers

15. Rob Lytle

16. First round

17. Curtis Greer

18. St. Louis Cardinals

19. Jim Harbaugh

20. Kevin Brooks

21. First round